Looking Through A Sandglass

Xena Aayesha Stephen

Presentation by *BookLeaf Publishing*

Web: www.bookleafpub.com

E-mail: info@bookleafpub.com

ISBN: 9789357745437

First edition 2023

ACKNOWLEDGEMENT

When I say that it all started in the spur of the moment, I wouldn't say that it is completely true. When the idea of getting published crossed my mind, Book Leaf Publishing, made it possible by providing the platform for showcasing my first published work. And, for that my gratitude for them is never ending.

Finally, I would like to acknowledge with gratitude, the love and support of my family- my parents, Aparna and Jerald; my brother, Richard. They were the supporters and believers who always made a path possible and kept me going, and without them this book would not have been possible.

Lost

When I look in those eyes,
I can see you trying so hard to hide the lies,
And I hate to trust them anymore.

I sometimes wonder,
That what had I done so wrong,
For you to treat me this way?

I try to put myself in your place,
Yet, I do not understand your reason to leave me,
I can never guess what's going on in that little head
of yours.

I suppose you always had that effect on me, for a
very long time,
But was just blinded by your sweet lies.

Do I ever cross your mind?
Even for once,
Am I a part of your life?
Or just a fragment, that will slowly fade away.

What am I to you?
Do you love me now, just the way you did years ago?
Or was it all a game to you?
A game we lose because you were too lost to find me.

Did we end well?
Or did we just end, to be well?

Will this interrogation,
End on a negotiation,
Or on a decision.

One that was made by me, and you,
And not just by me and a lost soul.

I will always be here, waiting,
For you to find me,
So that I can help you find yourself.

That is the only thought,
Tying us together,
In a bond that is meant to last forever.

But then I wonder,
Am I willing to help someone as lost as you?
And that too at the cost,
Of getting lost myself,
And causing for a bigger blunder.

So now I must make the choice,
In between you,
Or to pay heed to my inner voice,
That always knew.

Of all of the consequences,
That I must face,
For all the pretenses,
That I must embrace.

Forgiveness

Forgiveness was asked for the first time,
When Adam ate an apple from the forbidden tree,
He had asked for forgiveness for that crime,
And since then, man would seek for forgiveness to
free himself from misfortune.

What does forgiveness mean?
Is it when a man goes to a priest for confession?
Is it when a teen seeks for his mother's love?
Or is it when a man tries to persuade his woman as
his redemption?

What is the nature of forgiveness?
How does someone know that they are really
forgiven?
How does a man confessing or conversing with Jesus
in a church know whether he is forgiven?

How does someone know that they are forgiven?
We say that we seek for the truth and the meaning of
life,
But what do all these mean?

How can someone attain the supreme knowledge
through forgiveness?
How does God even forgive us or even know what it
is to be human?

I do not deny the fact that,
God did come in many forms on this earth;
But the nature of human is a diverse and complex
math.

God made us, but who are we to make him?
Who are we to divide him?

We are the smallest spec which could've been
forgotten in the vast space,
But it was He who gave us a life to live, a family to
call our own, and a place to call home.

Man is a selfish creature, and this cannot be changed,
And then there are things much bigger than this in the
world,
But being a smallest spec methodically arranged in
this vast universe,
All we can do is listen to His word,
And cleanse ourselves by asking for forgiveness.

Whispers of the Night Breeze

Soft as the satin silks,
Light as the cotton feathers,
Calm as the waves of the sea,
These are the whispers of the night breeze.

Warm as the hug from a loved one,
Breezy as the flutter of a beating heart,
Cool as the bearer of a triumph,
These are the whispers of the night breeze.

Caged to a confined space,
Free as the light rays,
Limited to a certain hour,
These are the whispers of the night breeze.

Calling to a certain soul,
Sharing a secret untold,
Wishing on a star for hope,
These are the whispers of the night breeze.

From a Ripple to a Tide

From a ripple to a tide,
An emotion impossible to hide,
As our hearts collide,
Intertwining into an inviolable bond.

From a ripple to a tide,
With you by my side,
An unfaltering heedful guide,
Unifying to create a future beyond.

From a ripple to a tide,
This moment of being satisfied,
As you swoop in and slide,
And take me to a fantasyland.

From a ripple to a tide,
I remember that I had cried,
When you had asked me to be your bride,
And I had known from that moment on.

You were the ripple to my tide.

The Colors of Emotions

They say grey,
Is the shade of my sadness,
But do they know,
That being blue is my true shade.

Just as they say,
You don't seem to be happy,
But do they know,
That being at my best is my true shade.

This is their way,
Of asking are you okay,
But do they know,
That being hurt is my true shade.

They want to try,
To understand my nature,
But do they know,
That being alone sometimes is my true shade.

When they try to pry,
Inside of my palette,
But do they know,
That being myself is my true shade.

When I say,
There is no right or wrong,
To the colors of emotions,
They will know,
That being you is your true shade.

You Have

You have shone on me like the glistening sun,
And bestowed me with the gift of life,
Given me everything and even more,
You have given me your breath and soul.

You made me in your likeness,
And gave me your kindness,
You have made me with joyfulness,
And created me with all of your goodness.

You have told me of the times of happiness,
And of all the times of sadness,
You have also taught me of faithfulness,
And reminded me of thankfulness.

You have taught me of your holy words,
Have been there when I needed you the most,
Gave me your love and affection,
You have given me your breath and soul.

Fall

I fall into the depths,
Not knowing,
When the bottom fast approaches me.

It seems like a hole,
A pit even, of nothingness,
Or is it just my imagination?

Whispers? No, voices,
They had called out to me,
They had promised me,
Of hope and brighter days.

On an intersection,
I had to make a decision,
But the voices,
Let me have no other choices.

They had led me down a marshy path,
That swirled and twisted,
Got dark and murky,
As I entered deep within.

I had known then,
This was not my road,
But the unseen force,
Dragged me deep into the forest.

I remember entering the woods,
In search of something,
Or was it someone?

I was at a point,
Of losing my sanity,
Or was I being paranoid,
And distorting my own reality.

I wonder whether if all of this is in my head,
Or it is just a fleeting nightmare,
And I am just sleeping on my bed,
But there was something about this nightmare that I
just couldn't bear.

And now, as I fall into the depths,
Not knowing,
When the bottom fast approaches me,
I only hope this nightmare comes to an end.

Silence

In the quiet you find a hurricane,
In the silence you obtain perspective,
And in solitude you discover purpose.

In the noise you gain your voice,
In the hubbub you search for aim,
And in company you uncover friendship.

A little difficult,
And a little subtle,
This is an art,
To pursue and master.

An art to befriend,
The friendship of silence,
And with patience,
You need not pretend.

For in silence you are the hurricane,
That has the strength to make a change,
To tame the raging storms,
And rearrange the strings of fate.

Broken Heart

I sing songs of the broken heart,
Melodies of the memories of the past,
But oh! This foolish heart,
Knows no bounds to Avast!

Of all the times of it was at ease,
This broken heart has stories,
And now it must witness,
The bitterness of anguish.

This broken heart,
When in pain,
Thumps against my chest,
Reminding me,
Of the burden it shoulders.

When I look over my shoulder,
And see the smile on your face,
And the way you act so colder,
When you are at my place.

But this broken heart,
Reminds me,
Of the good times
Of the warmth you radiated.
I smile to myself,
Knowing of what's to come next,
And that being selfish,
Is not for the best.

And I know,
If I let my heart rest,
This pain shall fade away,
So, I must let you go.

Dream

I am dream,
Some have me,
Some claim me.

There are some who dare to face me,
There are some who fear me.

Yet, all of them need me,
And must meet me,
At midnight.

I am dream,
You can't seize me,
Nor reproduce me.

You may have me,
In any way,
Your heart desires.

Big or small,
It is all,
In your imagination.

It is you,
That can affect,
Your own dream.

I am dream,
And I do not meddle,
With your destiny.

I am only the medium,
A corridor,
Who guides you,
When you sleep.

I am dream,
And I rise,
From within the shadows.

You shouldn't fear me,
For I am the intersection,
Between creation and success.

Night Sky

The night sky twinkles,
With millions of memories,
Of the past.

Each star casts,
With its shine,
A beautiful outline,
And a mesmerizing design.

The night sky twinkles,
With the reminiscences,
Of many a centuries.

Each star singing,
With its shine,
Of stories contrasting,
And shining brightest when together.

Sands of Time

Through the sands of time,
I wander in search of life,
To find purpose,
Or a mission,
But most of all,
A fragment of myself.

Though difficult a challenge,
I must conquer the dangers,
That lie in plain sight,
Finding their chance,
To grab hold of me.

Through the sands of time,
I must look within,
To search for the light,
That will guide me,
On this perilous expedition.

Though difficult a task,
I must face my fears,
And return home victorious,
And bring the light of hope,
To those with the same purpose.

Blossoms

When the blossoms bloomed,
Bringing with them,
Their scent and beauty,
Bejeweling nature with its tranquility.

When the blossoms bloomed,
It casted the air with its perfume,
And painted the streets,
With the shades of pink.

When the seasons transition,
An its time of the blossoms,
To wither and fall away.

It gives nature a redefinition,
And brings balance,
To the cycle of life.

You

You were a mystery,
That people had told me,
Was better locked away,
And hushed.

Out of curiosity,
I had only listened,
To my heart and its voice,
And shushed the people out.

You had inexplicably,
Risked and dared to,
Gone through my secrets.
And pushed me to never be afraid.

You had ultimately,
Become a part of me,
Which was better locked away,
In my heart.

Off-Course Of Course

Pull up the sails,
And scupper that booty,
Let us get ready,
To head off- course, of course.

Either reach the horizon,
Or become dead men who tell no tales,
So, savvy?
To head off course, of course.

Set sail to a mystical island,
Do not fear of what lies ahead,
So are you ready for a new expedition,
To head off-course, of course.

From Kraken, to sea beasts, to mermaids,
The myths aren't confined to the books laddie,
So, c'mon weigh anchor,
To head off-course, of course.

Grown Up

I had always anticipated,
Of being a grown up,
And of all the things I would achieve.

For the little me,
Knew much of nothing,
But had fictitious characters,
To look up to.

From princesses to superheroes,
I had wanted to be all of them,
And eventually, I was a grown up,
And they had never come to the rescue,
Nor ever showed up.

When I was in trouble,
Or was stuck up,
In the reality,
Of being a grown up.

Perfect Morning

The refreshing scent of coffee beans,
The sound of the kettle's whistle,
The bright rays of the sun,
Seeping through cotton curtains,
That is a perfect morning.

Birds singing the morning lullaby,
Streams casting their imprints on sand,
The light tint of the blue sky,
That is a perfect morning.

The winds humming the messages of peace,
The trees restoring the history of centuries,
This is what we believe,
To be a perfect morning.

To Be, To Find

When I was a kid,
I had a dream,
To be an astronaut,
Or to be a king,
To be omnipresent,
And save the day.

For when I was a kid,
I will surely admit,
My world was too big,
And imagination, endless.

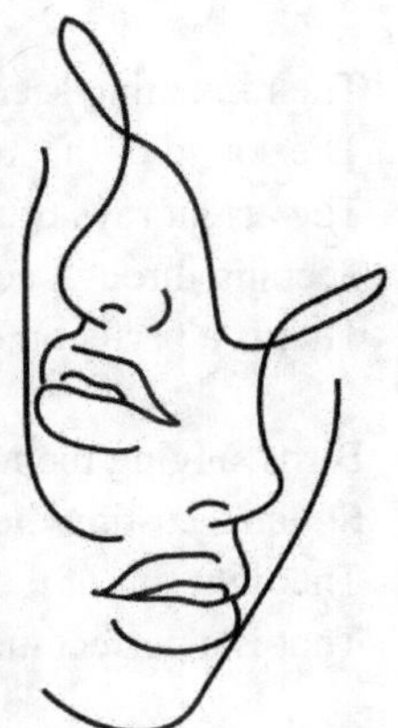

When I was a teen,
I had a dream,
To find who I am,
And have my own definition to life,
To save myself from presumptions.

When I entered into adulthood,
I had the dream,
To find something to call my own,
To grab onto hope,
And have better days in life,
To save my face and make my own decisions.

Be Different

When you find,
The true meaning,
Of being different,
It is difficult to comprehend,
Or to even confess,
Of its true meaning,
And its depth.

When you hear,
People asking you,
To be different,
But to be yourself at the same time,
It is difficult to comprehend,
Or to even profess,
Of the true explanation,
And its complexity.

When you understand,
What it truly means,
To be different,
And to find your voice at the same time,
You come to appreciate and accept,
Of not being afraid,
And interpret,
The simplicity and become different.

Someone

We all have that someone,
Whom we just connect with,
On a different level,
Of intimacy and understanding.

That someone who knows you,
With the weirdness and loudness,
Accepts and cherishes you,
And still keeps standing beside you,
Through thick and thin.

This someone needn't always be,
A romantic interest,
It can just be,
Someone who is interested,
And enjoys your company,
Even during the good times,
And becomes your anchor,
During those bad times.

Through a Sandglass

27

The view that I had,
To the perceptions that were discovered,
For a while I had the chance,
To look within my own self,
Through a sandglass.

To feelings that were left unspoken,
And secrets that were hidden,
For a while I had the courage,
Of letting go of the fear to look,
Through a sandglass.

And when I enclose these words,
Within the pages of time,
I shall know that I had the chance,
To encounter and glance at myself,
Through a sandglass.

www.ingramcontent.com/pod-product-compliance
Lightning Source LLC
LaVergne TN
LVHW021350200726
843509LV00014B/2770